108

MIGHTY MACHINES

Earth Movers

by M. T. Martin

BELLWETHER MEDIA • MINNEAPOLIS, MN

Note to Librarians, Teachers, and Parents:

Blastoff! Readers are carefully developed by literacy experts and combine standards-based content with developmentally appropriate text.

Level 1 provides the most support through repetition of high-frequency words, light text, predictable sentence patterns, and strong visual support.

Level 2 offers early readers a bit more challenge through varied simple sentences, increased text load, and less repetition of high-frequency words.

Level 3 advances early-fluent readers toward fluency through increased text and concept load, less reliance on visuals, longer sentences, and more literary language.

Whichever book is right for your reader, Blastoff! Readers are the perfect books to build confidence and encourage a love of reading that will last a lifetime!

This edition first published in 2007 by Bellwether Media.

No part of this publication may be reproduced in whole or in part without written permission of the publisher. For information regarding permission, write to Bellwether Media Inc., Attention: Permissions Department, Post Office Box 1C, Minnetonka, MN 55345-9998.

Library of Congress Cataloging-in-Publication Data
Martin, M. T. (Martin Theodore)
  Earth movers / by M. T. Martin.
     p. cm. — (Blastoff! readers) (Mighty machines)
Summary: "Simple text and supportive images introduce young readers to earth movers. Intended for students in kindergarten through third grade."
  Includes bibliographical references and index.
  ISBN-10: 1-60014-047-5 (hardcover : alk. paper)
  ISBN-13: 978-1-60014-047-1 (hardcover : alk. paper)
  1. Excavating machinery—Juvenile literature. 2. Earthwork—Juvenile literature. I. Title.
II. Series. III. Series: Mighty machines (Bellwether Media)

TA735.M3878 2006
  624.1'52—dc22   2006007215

Text copyright © 2007 by Bellwether Media.
Printed in the United States of America.

Table of Contents

An earth mover
digs up dirt.

An earth mover
carries dirt.

An earth mover dumps dirt. Then the earth mover goes back for another **load**.

This earth
mover is
a **scraper**.

631E

Scrapers carry dirt in large **cans**.

631E

can

13

This earth
mover is
a **loader**.

Loaders carry dirt in large **buckets**.

bucket

An earth mover
has a **cab**.
A **driver** sits
in the cab.

An earth mover
is a big machine.
It can move a lot
of dirt.

Glossary

bucket—a large scoop for holding dirt on an earth mover

cab—a place for the driver to sit

can—a large space for holding dirt on an earth mover

driver—a person who runs a machine

load—anything that is carried or lifted by a machine or a person

loader—an earth mover that uses a large bucket to carry dirt

scraper—an earth mover that uses a blade to dig and a can to carry dirt

To Learn More

AT THE LIBRARY

Kalman, Bobbie. *Dirt Movers*. New York: Crabtree Publishing Company, 1994.

Rogers, Hal. *Earthmovers*. Eden Prairie, Minn.: The Child's World, Inc., 1998.

Williams, Linda, D. *Earthmovers*. Mankato, Minn: Capstone Press, 2005.

ON THE WEB

Learning more about mighty machines is as easy as 1, 2, 3.

1. Go to www.factsurfer.com

2. Enter "mighty machines" into search box.

3. Click the "Surf" button and you will see a list of related web sites.

With factsurfer.com, finding more information is just a click away.

Index

The photographs in this book are reproduced with the permission of: Deere, Inc., front cover, pp. 4-5, 6-7, 8-9, 14-15, 16-17, 18-19; Juan Martinez, pp. 10-11, 12-13; Marcus Lyon/Getty Images, pp. 20-21.